Children's Ministry Clip Art

Illustrations by Mary Lynn Ulrich

Group Books

Loveland, Colorado

Dedication

To Mike for all your love and support.
To my students—thanks for all your goofy faces and inspirations.

Children's Ministry Clip Art

Copyright © 1990 by Mary Lynn Ulrich

First Printing

Credits
Edited by Jolene L. Roehlkepartain
Cover design by Judy Atwood Bienick

Library of Congress Cataloging-in-Publication Data

Ulrich, Mary Lynn, 1965-
Children's ministry clip art / illustrations by Mary Lynn Ulrich.
p.   cm.
Includes index.
ISBN 1-55945-018-5
1. Church work with children. 2. Copy art. I. Title.
BV 639.C4 1990   90-35301
259'.22'028—dc20   CIP
Printed in the United States of America

Contents

Introduction
25 Ways to Use Clip Art Creatively

Boost interest in your children's ministry with *Children's Ministry Clip Art*. This book contains more than 300 pieces of art that'll grab children's attention.

The book contains designs from animals to food to program topics to monthly calendars that'll help you produce attractive—yet inexpensive—publicity for children's ministry.

So be creative. Think of ways to use this book, starting with:

1. Newsletters—Start a newsletter for kids. Or write a regular page in your church newsletter. Publish information about upcoming events and news about individual children. Sprinkle it with fun art. Include a monthly calendar parents and children can post at home (page 104).

2. Fliers—Announce future children's ministry and Sunday school events by giving pertinent information. (See "Clip-Art Basics.") Add illustrations to grab people's attention.

3. Handouts—Spiff up handouts by adding attractive designs from this clip-art book.

4. Bulletin inserts—Announce a new event with pizazz. Find an illustration that emphasizes your message and add it to a bulletin insert.

5. Coloring sheets—Enlarge clip-art illustrations so younger kids can color them.

6. Posters—Enlarge an image or two to make posters for an upcoming meeting. Use the "Tantalizing Topics" (page 36) that fit your theme.

7. Collages—Photocopy clip-art pictures and let kids cut them out. Then have them paste different images on a sheet of paper to form a collage of their interests. See "Tantalizing Topics" (page 36) and "Great Games and Super Sports" (page 60) for starters.

8. Name tags—Find a piece of clip art to photocopy and use for name tags. For example, use "Furry Friends and Other Beasts" (page 72) when you're making name tags for a meeting with an animal theme.

9. Place cards—If you're having a dinner or Sunday school breakfast, make place cards by using "All Kinds of Kids" (page 66). Write each child's name on a separate place card.

10. Bulletin boards—Enlarge a monthly calendar from "Creative Calendars" (page 10). Then make an attractive bulletin board. Decorate it with seasonal art from "Holidays, Holy Days and Other Special Days" (page 81).

11. Logos—Find a logo for your children's ministry and photocopy it to use for posters, handouts, name tags and stationery for your children to use.

12. Greeting cards—Photocopy birthday designs or other important greetings onto construction paper. Then fold the paper to make cards to mail to children.

13. Wall murals—Find a design you'd like to paint on your wall. Trace it onto the wall using an overhead projector. Then paint your original decor.

14. Place mats—Enlarge images from "Fun Foods, Fund-Raisers and Service Projects" (page 28). Paste each image on a piece of construction paper. Ask kids to color and decorate them. Then use the place mats for a church dinner.

15. Mobiles—Photocopy a bunch of designs and let kids color them, cut them out and paste them to construction paper. Then have them use string to hang the images from hangers to make mobiles.

16. Invitations—Use clip art to make invitations for parties, parent teas and other special children's ministry events.

17. Personalized stationery—Instead of using church stationery for the letters you mail to parents and volunteers, make your own stationery by using clip art. Choose a design from "Magnificent Motifs for Ministry" (page 7) and have a local quick printer print your stationery.

18. Calendars—Each month, photocopy a monthly calendar from "Creative Calendars" (page 104). Type meeting times and special events in the appropriate sections. Then photocopy the calendar and mail it to parents before the beginning of each month.

19. Puzzles—Enlarge clip-art illustrations and cut them into pieces. Have kids put the puzzle pieces together.

20. Stick puppets—Photocopy clip art from "All Kinds of Kids" (page 66) and "Furry Friends and Other Beasts" (page 72). Have kids color the pictures, cut them out and glue them to Popsicle sticks. Add construction paper backings for strength. Then have kids put on a puppet show.

21. Advertising—When advertising your children's ministry or Sunday school in your community newspaper, use clip art to make the ads more attractive.

22. T-shirts—Find a design from this clip-art book and have an artist from your church silk screen the design on T-shirts for your kids.

23. Tickets—Instead of buying tickets to sell for children's ministry events, make your own tickets using clip art.

24. Stickers—Buy adhesive-back photocopy paper and photocopy clip art onto it. Then cut out the designs to make stickers.

25. Bookmarks—Make bookmarks from heavy construction paper by using clip art. Print a scripture on each bookmark. Then punch a hole at the top and add a yarn tassel.

Clip-Art Basics

To use clip art effectively, follow these steps:

● Decide what you need to publicize. For example, do you need to get the word out about vacation Bible school?

● Choose how you want to publicize the event. You may want to mail a flier or decorate a bulletin board.

● Write a rough draft of what you want to say. Include pertinent information such as who, what, when, what time, where, why and cost. Be sure to include your name and telephone number.

● Thumb through this book and find designs that fit the occasion and capture attention.

● Cut out pictures and words you want to use. If the items are too small or too large, enlarge or reduce them with a photocopy machine.

● Type all the information you need on a blank sheet of paper. Then secure the art, words and titles to the paper with rubber cement.

● Now just photocopy and mail your flier. Your publicity is finished!

Magnificent Motifs for Ministry

1 2 3

1 2 3

abc

abc

preschool

preschool

preschool

1 2 3

abc

kindergarten

kindergarten

Kindergarten

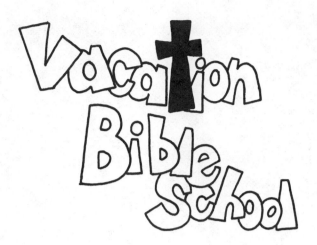

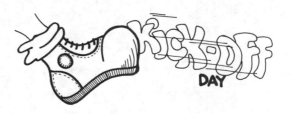

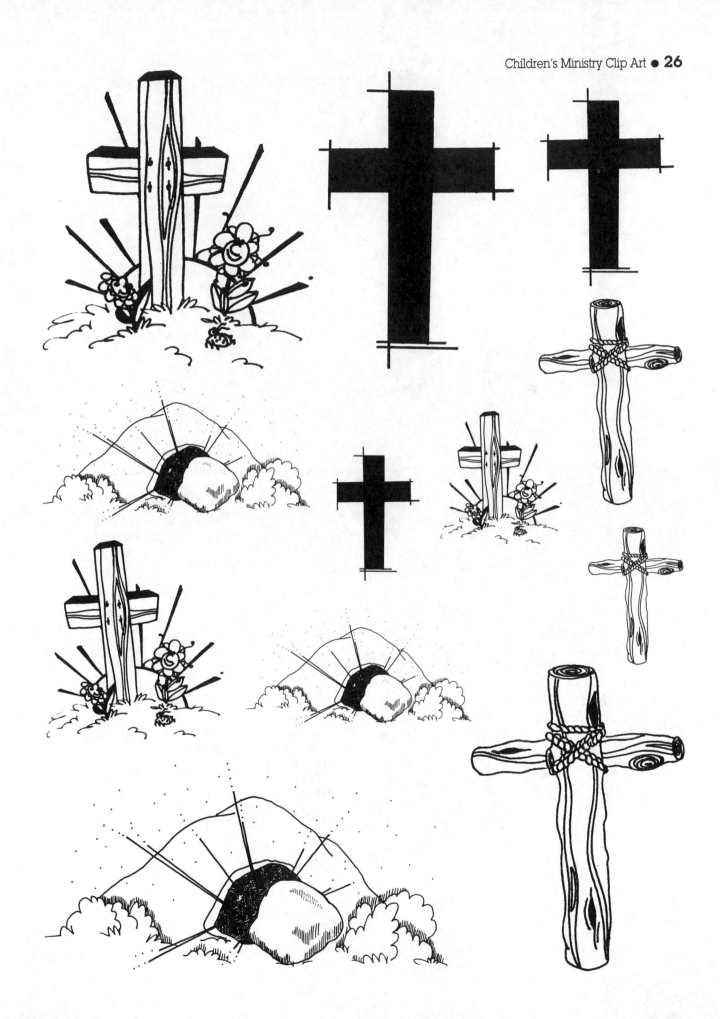

Fun Food, Fund-Raisers and Service Projects

Service PROJECT

Nursing Home Visitation

Nursing Home Visitation

Service PROJECT

Service PROJECT

Nursing Home Visitation

Tantalizing Topics

bullies

bullies

bullies

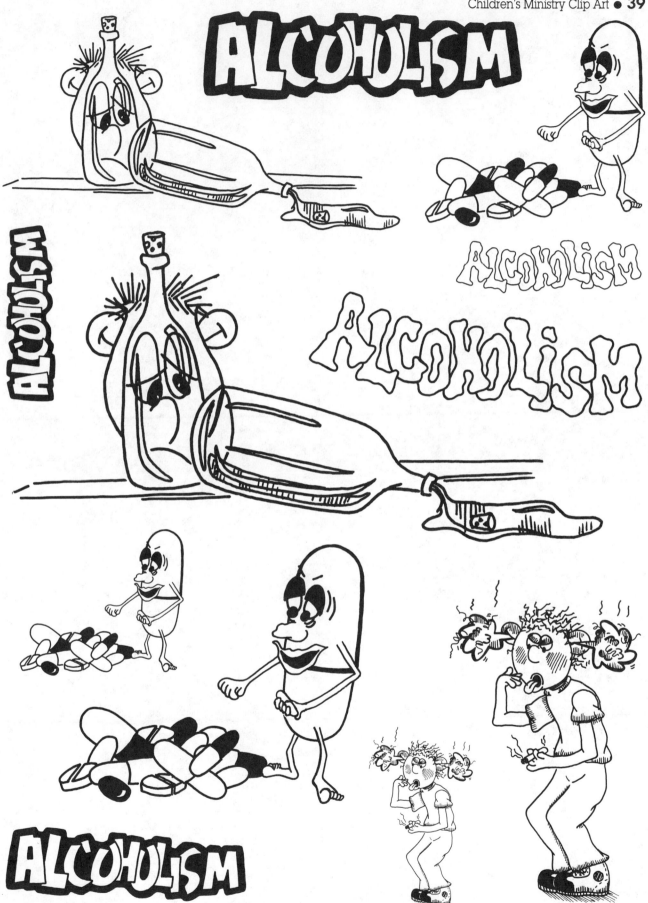

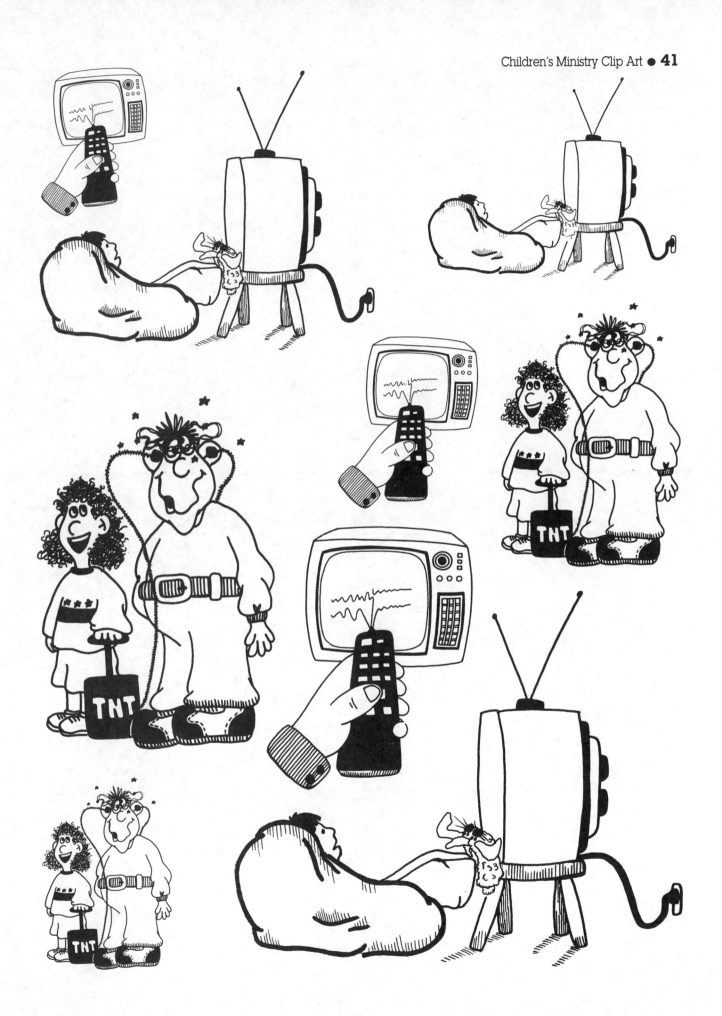

Basic Bible Stories

Adam and Eve

Noah's Ark

The Plagues in Egypt

Adam and Eve

Noah's Ark

The Plagues in Egypt

Jesus the Good Shepherd

David and Goliath

David and Goliath

David and Goliath

The Ten Commandments

The Ten Commandments

Jesus the Good Shepherd

Jesus the Good Shepherd

The Ten Commandments

Daniel in the Lions' Den

Jesus' Birth

Jesus' Birth

Jonah and the Whale

Jonah and the Whale

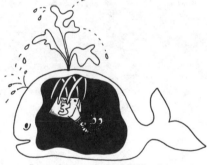

Jonah and the Whale

Daniel in the Lions' Den

Daniel in the Lions' Den

Jesus' Birth

Jesus Walking on Water

Feeding the 5,000

Boy Jesus in the Temple

Boy Jesus in the Temple

Jesus Walking on Water

Feeding the 5,000

Feeding the 5,000

Jesus Walking on Water

Boy Jesus in the Temple

Jesus With Children

The Prodigal Son

The Good Samaritan

Jesus With Children

The Good Samaritan

The Prodigal Son

The Good Samaritan

The Prodigal Son

Jesus With Children

Paul Set Free From Prison

Paul Set Free From Prison

Jesus Changing Water to Wine

Paul in Prison

Stephen's Stoning

Jesus Changing Water to Wine

Paul in Prison

Appreciations and Affirmations

Parent-Appreciation Night

Parent-Appreciation Night

UNLIMITED USE PLEASE

COUPON GOOD FOR...

HUGS

UNLIMITED USE FOR THE COUPON HOLDER!

REDEEM ANYTIME

UNLIMITED USE PLEASE

COUPON GOOD FOR...

HUGS

UNLIMITED USE FOR THE COUPON HOLDER!

REDEEM ANYTIME

Parent-Appreciation Night

Parent-Appreciation Night

UNLIMITED USE PLEASE

COUPON GOOD FOR...

HUGS

UNLIMITED USE FOR THE COUPON HOLDER!

REDEEM ANYTIME

Parent-Appreciation Night

Parent-Appreciation Night

Great Games and Super Sports

Soccer

Soccer

Soccer

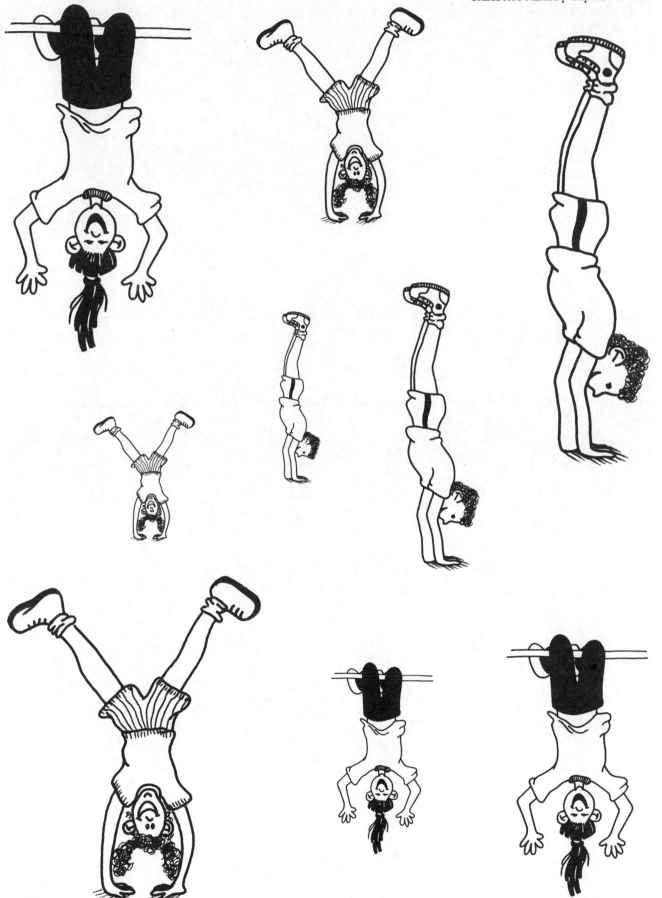

All Kinds of Kids

Furry Friends and Other Beasts

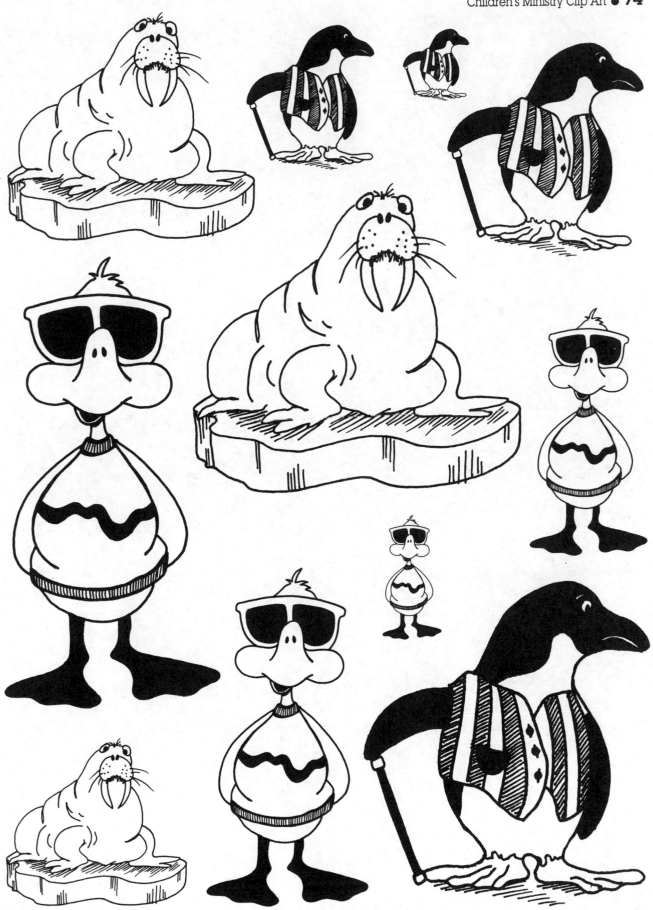

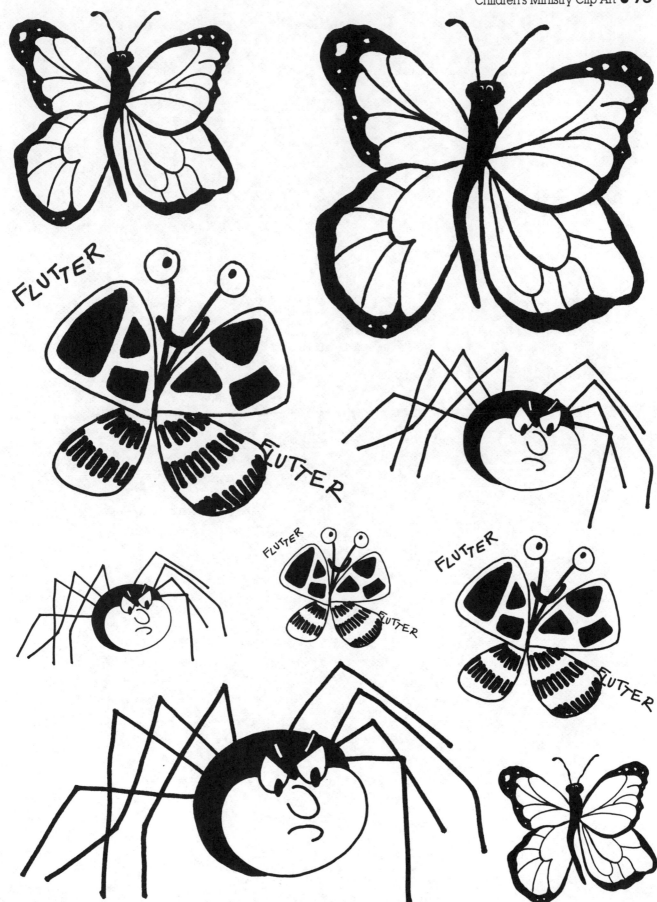

FLUTTER

FLUTTER

FLUTTER

FLUTTER

FLUTTER

FLUTTER

Holidays, Holy Days and Other Special Days

happy Valentine's Day

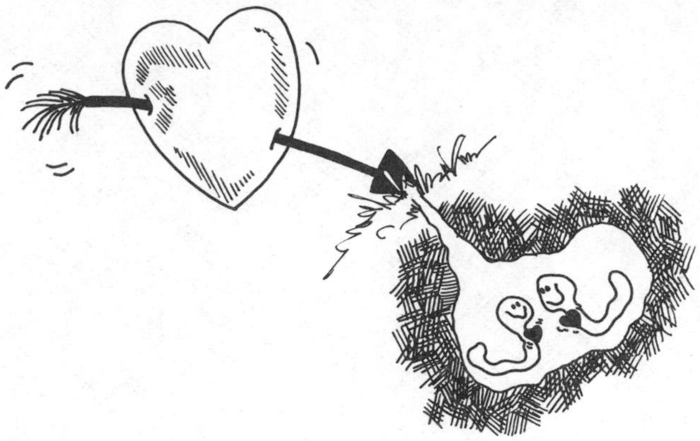

happy Valentine's Day

happy Valentine's Day

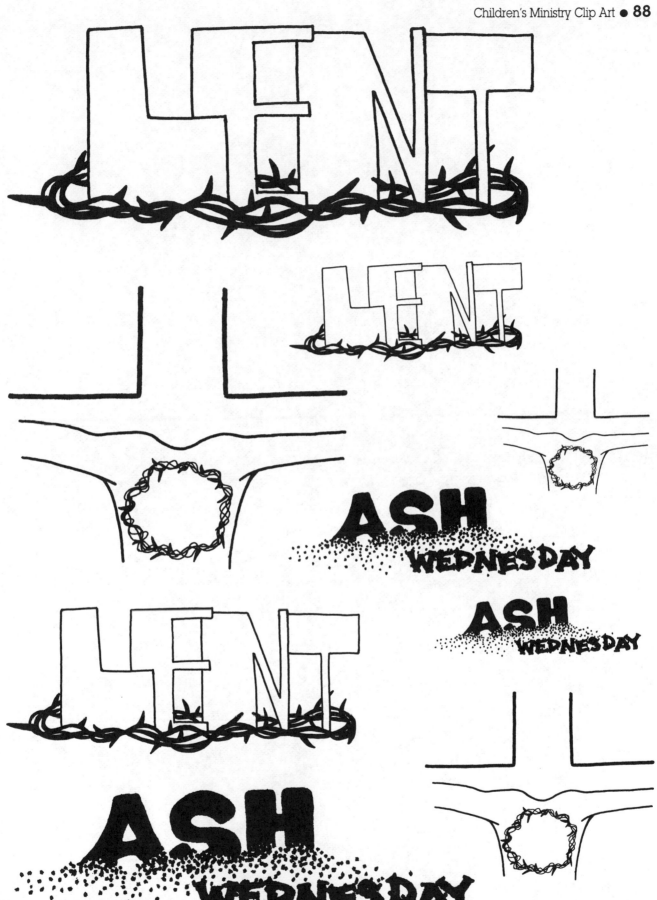

Good Friday

he is risen!

Good Friday

he is risen!

Good Friday

he is risen!

APRIL **FOOLS'** DAY

APRIL **FOOLS'** DAY

APRIL **FOOLS'** DAY

Hurray
for
Summer

Hurray
for
Summer

memorial
day

memorial
day

Hurray
for
Summer

memorial
day

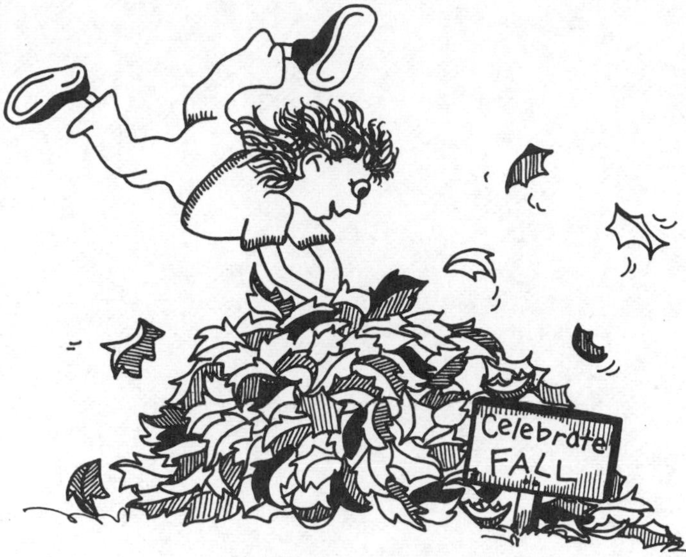
Celebrate
FALL

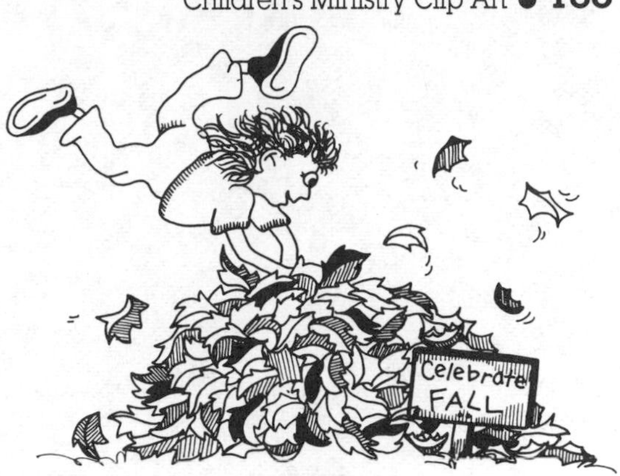
Celebrate
FALL

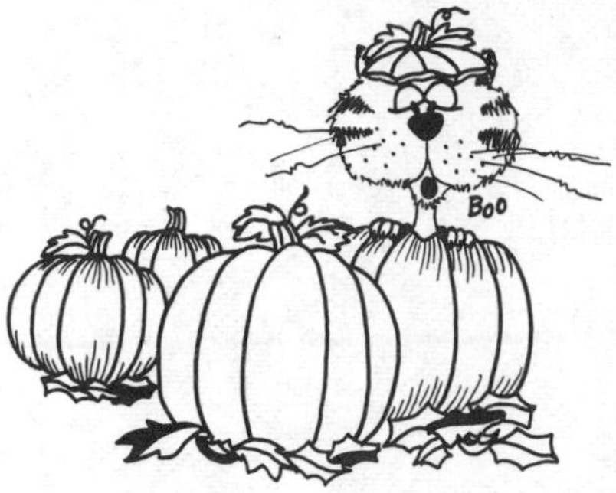
Boo

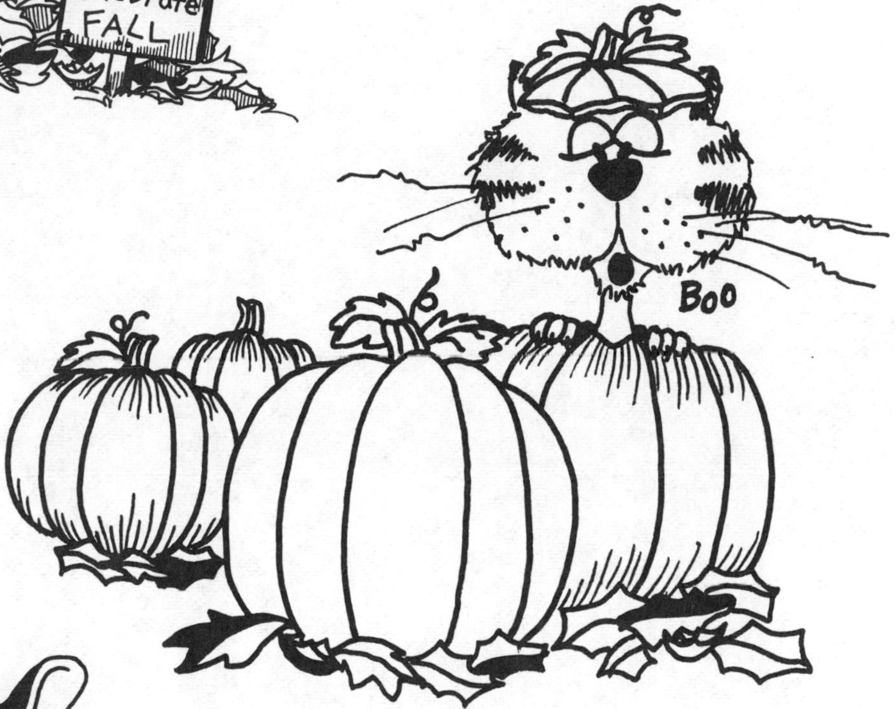
Boo

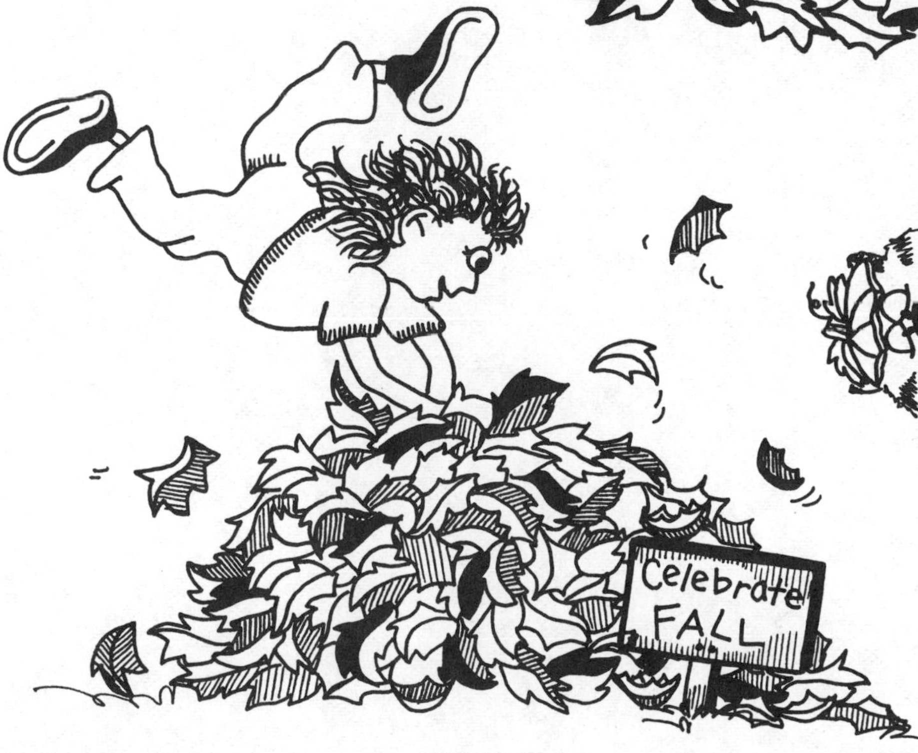
Celebrate
FALL

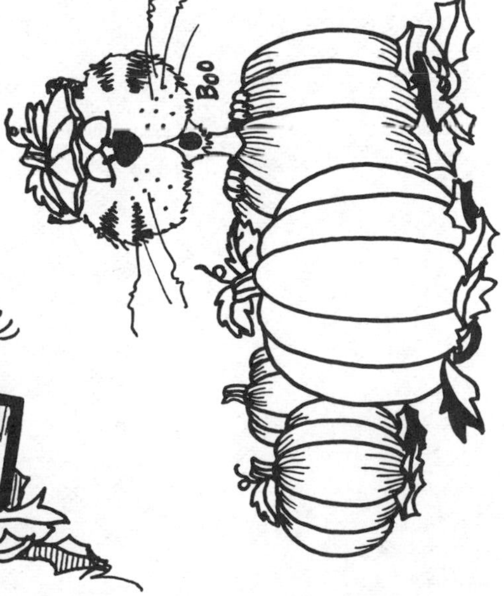
Boo

Creative Calendars

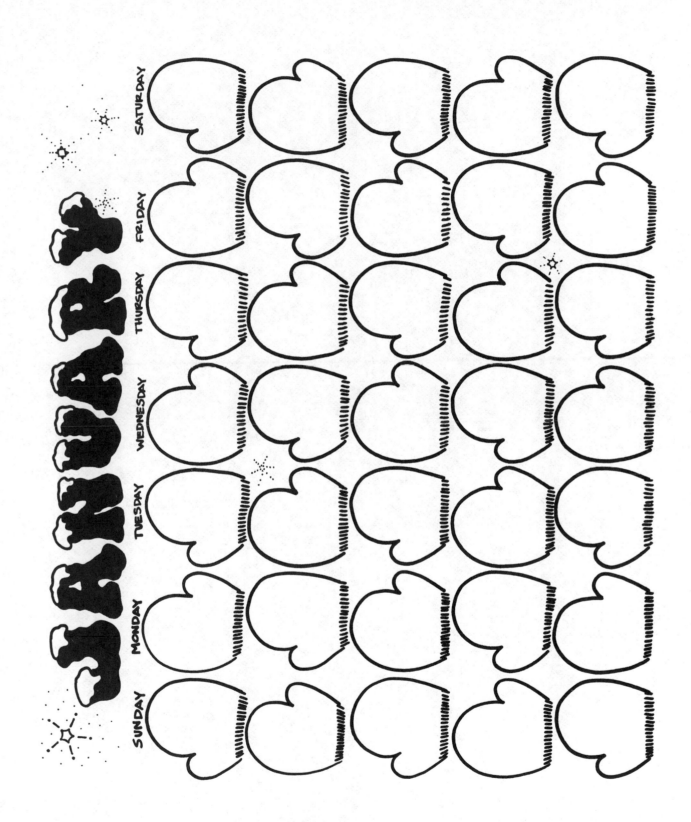

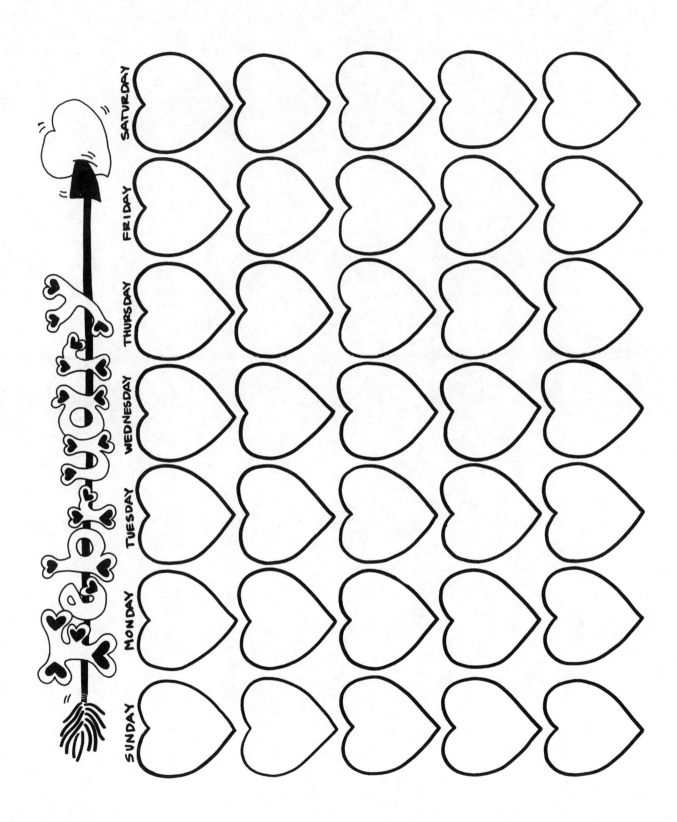

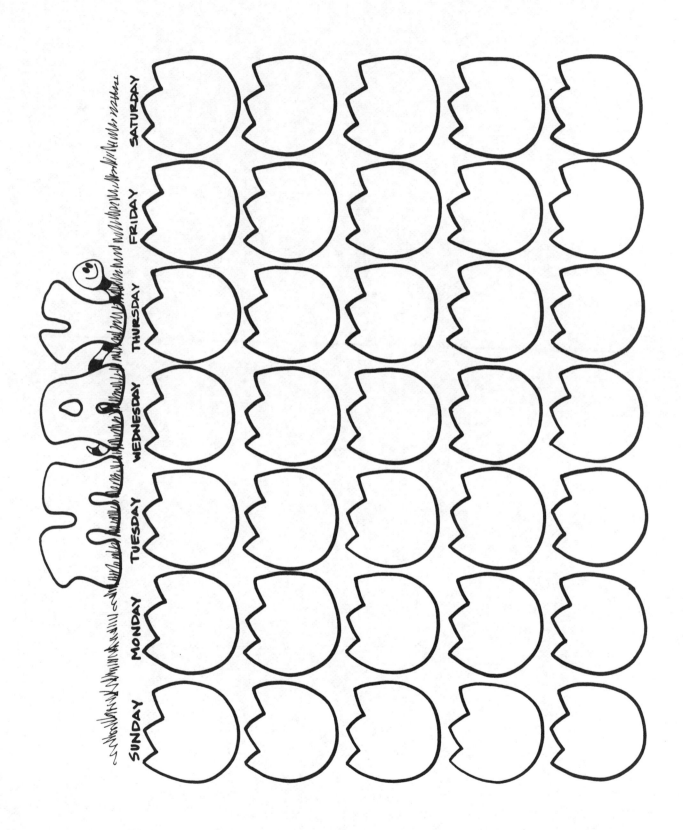

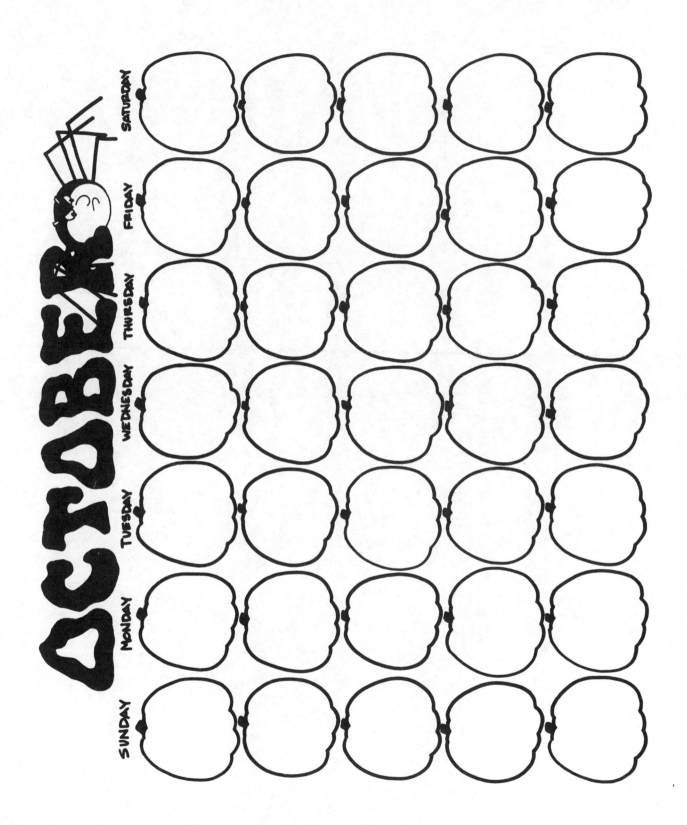

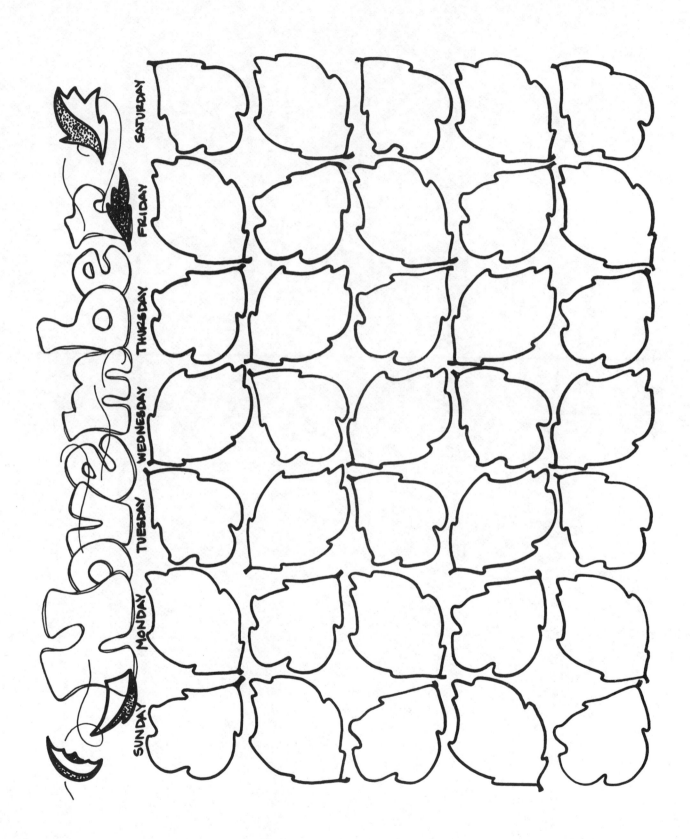

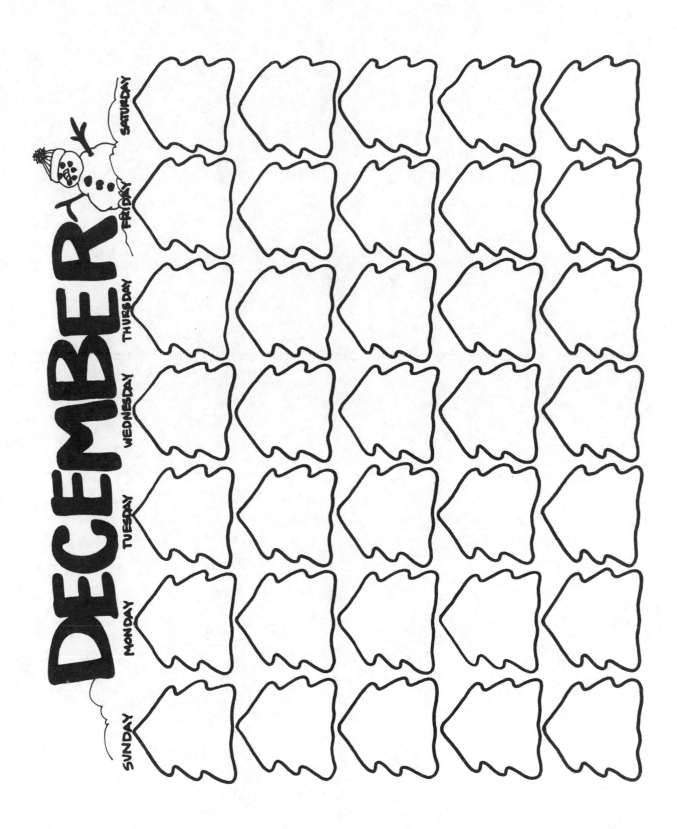

Signs and Sayings

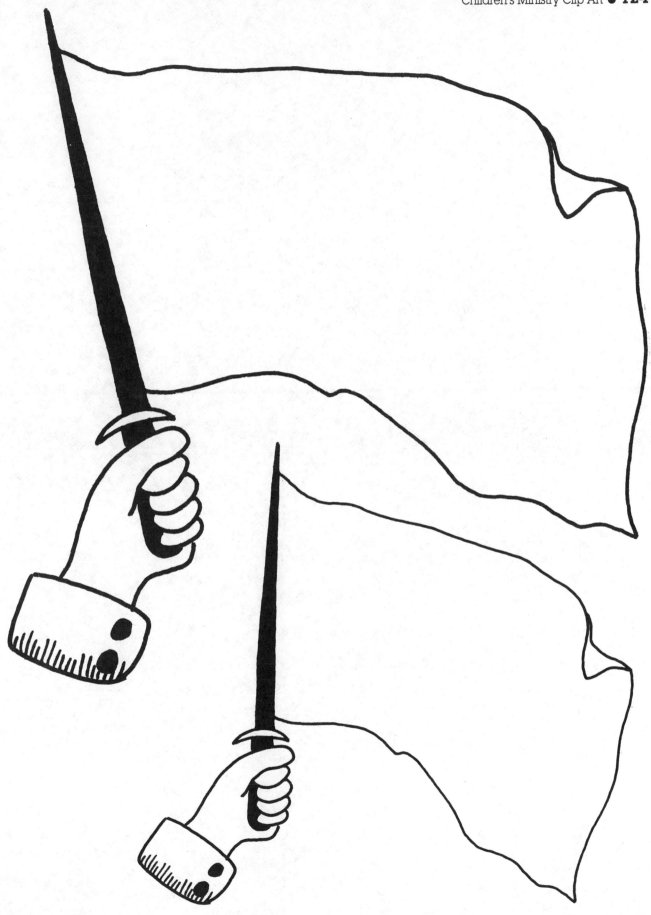

WHAT'S UP?

GOOD JOB

Bring Your Friends

REGISTER   ARRIVING: TAKE NOTE

COST: TIME: SPEAKER

WONDERFUL   COOL

You're Great   JOIN US   Bummer

1 2 3 4 5 6 7 8 9 0

TERRIFIC

Bad   GREAT

WHEE!

CONGRATULATIONS

Yippee!   GET WELL

1 2 3 4 5 6 7 8 9 0   FUN

DON'T FORGET   SURPRISE

NOW SHOWING   YUCK

BRING YOUR FRIENDS   Good

COMING SOON

1 2 3 4 5 6 7 8 9 0

Place: **FIELD TRIP** *WOW!*

HOW MUCH? Out Of This World! **Bum Deal**

Mark Your Calendar JOY

NEAT WHY? *NEW*

Peace THANKS KOWABUNGA!

Cost Includes: WE MISS YOU

DATE: **Don't Miss It!**

January	**April**	**July**	**October**
February	**May**	**August**	**November**
March	**June**	**September**	**December**

Sunday MARCH WHERE?

Monday Hooray WHAT?

Tuesday DEPARTING:

Wednesday WHEN? First-Class

Thursday Sign Up FIRE UP!

Information

Friday Welcome Goofy

Saturday Announcements

1 2 3 4 5 6 7 8 9 0

1 2 3 4 5 6 7 8 9 0

1 2 3 4 5 6 7 8 9 0

1 2 3 4 5 6 7 8 9 0 SORRY

WHAT'S DOWN? Awesome

Index